Granuaile

CHIEFTAIN, PIRATE, TRADER

GRACE O'MALLEY (Granuaile) was a bold independent leader. She was a Gaelic chieftain who lived under the ancient Brehon system and owned islands, castles and a fleet of ships. Her family traded with France, Spain, England and Portugal.

THE AUTHORS

Mary Moriarty lives in Dublin with her husband and three children. She took a degree with the Open University in arts and has taught in the Adult Literacy scheme in Dun Laoghaire.

Catherine Sweeney took a degree in arts at UCD. She has worked as a teacher at secondary level and as a translator and interpreter. She lives with her husband and children in Dublin.

GRACE O'MALLEY

GRANUAILE

CHIEFTAIN, PIRATE, TRADER

MARY MORIARTY
CATHERINE SWEENEY

Drawings David Rooney

THE O'BRIEN PRESS
DUBLIN

First published 1988 by The O'Brien Press Ltd.,
20 Victoria Road, Rathgar, Dublin 6, Ireland.
Copyright © text Mary Moriarty and Catherine Sweeney
Drawings © The O'Brien Press.

2 4 6 8 10 9 7 5 3

96 98 00 02 04 03 01 99 97 95

British Library Cataloguing-in-Publication Data
Moriarty, Mary
Granuaile
1. Ireland. O'Malley, Grace, 1530-1600
Biographies
I. Title II. Sweeney, Catherine
941.505'092'4

ISBN 0-86278-162-0

Editing, design, typesetting, layout: The O'Brien Press
Cover illustration: Brian Fitzgerald
Printing: The Guernsey Press Ltd

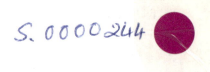

Contents

In the year 1530 a daughter was born to an Irish chieftain, Owen O'Malley, and his wife Margaret. They called her Grace. She was to grow up to become one of the most remarkable women in the history of Ireland.

The O'Malleys were a wealthy, seafaring clan. Their territory lay in Mayo in the west of Ireland and consisted of the land around Clew Bay and the islands in the Bay. They owned several castles in the area where the present towns of Westport and Louisburg are, as well as a castle on Clare Island which they used as their summer residence.

Although by the time of Grace's birth it was nearly 400 years since the Norman invasion of Ireland, life for an Irish family like the O'Malleys went on much the same as it had always done in the centuries before the Normans came. During the time of Grace's childhood — the 1530s and 1540s — English rule in Ireland was limited to an area of about 30 miles around Dublin and to the few towns that existed in Ireland at that time, Waterford, Wexford, Cork and Galway. The rest of the country was controlled by native Irish clans like Grace's family and by the descendants of the Norman invaders who were called the Anglo-Irish. Many of the Anglo-Irish by this time had adopted the Irish language, customs and laws and become 'more Irish than the Irish themselves'. In the Ireland of Grace's childhood therefore most of the people lived according to the old Gaelic customs and life-style and were to a large extent unaffected by the English administration.

Grace's father was a tall, strong, black-haired

Map of Ireland showing the great clans in the early sixteenth cent
None lived within the Pale.

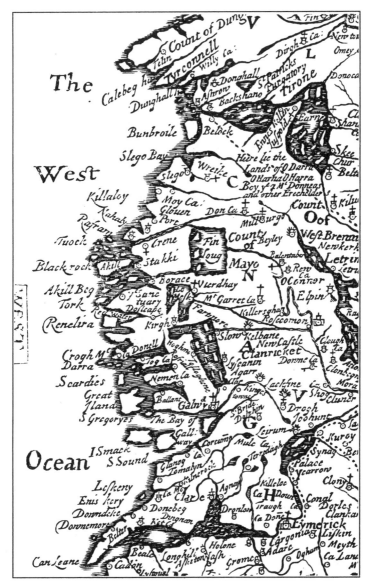

Map of Connaught, drawn up under the instructions of
Elizabeth I and published later in 1633.

man called Owen 'Dubhdarra' (Black Oak) O'Malley. Her mother, Margaret, was also an O'Malley, coming from a different branch of the family. Grace, like her father, was black-haired and dark-skinned. She grew up to be strong like him too.

SEAFARING

The O'Malleys' life was exciting and varied. Their main activity was seafaring and they owned a large fleet of ships. Fishing was their main source of wealth. They controlled all the fishing around Clew Bay and French and Spanish fishing fleets wanting to fish the area had to pay the O'Malleys for permission. The O'Malleys were very experienced sailors and every year sailed to places as far away as Spain and Portugal on trading expeditions. These journeys required great skill in those days when they had only basic navigational aids and the seas were infested with pirates. On their trips to Spain the O'Malleys took fish, hides, wool and linen as cargo and traded them in Spain for products that were not available in Ireland like wine, silks and spices. Latin was their second language and as this would have been understood by the Spaniards they had no language problems. In Grace's time the languages spoken by the native Irish ruling class were Irish and Latin. Grace must have accompanied her father on many of his trips to Spain learning to navigate and command a ship because she later became known as a 'most famous feminine sea captain'.

DAY-TO-DAY LIFE

Grace's main home when she was growing up was Belclare Castle — a stone, tower-like building.

Grace loved to play cards — one of her nicknames
was 'Grace of the Gamblers'.

There are still remains of tower-castles from this time in different parts of Ireland and they seem very bleak places to live. However, in Grace's time, they would have been full of people, with a roaring log fire in their great hall, sheepskins on the walls and floors and perhaps furnishings acquired on their regular trading trips to Spain.

Life at Belclare was a crowded, busy affair. Grace had one brother called Donal-na-Piopa (Donal of the Pipes). She would never have been lonely because in those days the chieftain's lands belonged to the whole clan. Grace would therefore have grown up surrounded by cousins, aunts, uncles and other relations. There would have been a constant stream of visitors as there was a strong tradition of hospitality in the Gaelic way of life and every visitor was offered a meal and a place to sleep.

The main pastimes in those days were card-playing, music and story-telling. Grace was very fond of and very good at playing cards. In fact one of her nicknames was Granna-na-gCearbhach (Grace of the Gamblers). Professional card-players called *carrows* would roam the country looking for gaming partners. It was said that they would gamble away their lands, clothes and even their finger and toe-nails!

Every chieftain had his own *file* or poet who would compose poetry for feasts, battles and raids and who would recite the ancient legends of Ireland. These *fili* were held in great respect, ranking second only to the chieftain. No-one dared offend these poets for fear that they would be mocked or criticised in one of their poems.

Hunting was another favourite activity and a profitable one as the hillsides at that time were full

*Stone plaque in Clare Island Abbey engraved with the O'Malley
coat of arms and the family motto.*

of wild animals, especially large red deer.

The O'Malleys possessed large herds of cattle and sheep and every summer the whole family and household moved to Clare Island to provide summer grazing for the herds. This movement to summer pastures, called *booleying*, was an old Gaelic custom dating back hundreds of years. We can imagine that Grace must have looked forward to her summer stay on Clare Island as temporary houses were erected every summer for living in and most of the cooking and eating were done out-of-doors.

Alongside the peaceful occupations of fishing, cattle-rearing and trading, the O'Malleys also engaged in more war-like activities. Life in sixteenth-century Ireland could be violent and dangerous and chieftains regularly raided each other's territories taking away cattle, possessions and sometimes even members of each other's clans. The O'Malleys were no exception. They had an advantage over more inland clans in that they could strike from sea and withdraw to Clew Bay where nobody could follow them as they owned Clare Island at the entry to the Bay and all the land surrounding the Bay. They lived up to the motto of the O'Malley clan, *Terra marique potens* (powerful on land and sea).

Grace spent her childhood in Belclare Castle and on Clare Island. She would have been baptised and have attended Mass in Murrisk Abbey near her home at Belclare. This monastery was built for the monks by the O'Malley family in 1457. She would have accompanied her father on his sailing trips and helped her mother with the many tasks involved in running the large household at Belclare. These tasks included organising the women workers in spinning and weaving clothes for the family,

Upset when her father refused to take her on a trip because she was a girl, the story goes that Grace cut off her hair and donned male clothes.

and in supervising the preparation and serving of the meals for the many castle residents.

From a story that is told about how she got her name, we can imagine that Grace preferred trips with her father to work in the household. According to the story, as a child she wanted to go on a trip with her father and brother. Her father told her that she could not go because she was a girl. She was very upset at this and ran away by herself. Just as her father was about to depart she reappeared with all her hair cut off and dressed like a boy. 'Now will you take me?' she said. Her parents were aghast at her appearance but her brother laughed at the funny spectacle of the short hair of the little girl and teased her with the words 'Grainne Mhaol', which means Bald Grace in Irish and so the story goes that is how she became Granuaile.

MARRIAGE

Once Grace entered her teens her parents would have begun looking for a suitable husband for her. In those days girls married early and the marriages were arranged by the parents. Because of the constant warfare between the different clans it was important for the chieftains to have rich and powerful friends to help them in times of attack. Marriages between clans were used to create such alliances and friendships. So Grace's parents would have been looking for a husband for her from among the sons of powerful neighbouring clans. They finally decided on Donal O'Flaherty, the son of the chieftain of the O'Flaherty clan. This was a good choice because the O'Flahertys were rulers of West Connaught, owning vast tracts of land stretching south from the O'Malley borders. Like the O'Malleys, the

*The Great Hall at Bunratty Castle. The O'Flaherty hall at
Bunowen probably looked very like this.*

O'Flahertys were great seafarers. This would have
appealed to Grace with her love of the sea. Donal
was also *Tanaist* or heir to the Chief of the O'Flahertys.

The marriage took place in 1546 when Grace was 16. She may have been married in the monastery near her home. The wedding ceremony would have been followed by an enormous banquet and celebrations which probably lasted several days. When all the feasting and revelry was over Donal and Grace set out for their new home in O'Flaherty territory. They probably made the journey by sea as there were few roads in Connaught at the time. We can only wonder what the 16-year-old Grace's thoughts were as she sailed away to her new life. She would have known it was not going to be an entirely peaceful life because Donal's nickname was Donal-an-Chogaidh, Donal of the Battles. He was given this name because of his fiery temperament and warring nature.

On his marriage, Donal was given two homes. One was the Castle of Bunowen and the other a fortress at Ballinahinch.

Donal and Grace set up home at Bunowen. The castle stood beside a well-concealed inlet quite near Slyne Head. It was perfectly situated as it was out of sight of the main shipping area. Fear of the treacherous waters or of being trapped and looted kept strange ships away. Bunowen was tucked away between the sea, the Twelve Bens mountains and the wild beautiful scenery of Connemara.

As far as we know Grace settled down to her domestic duties. She and Donal had two sons Owen and Murrough and a daughter Margaret. Bringing up three children and running two castles obviously kept Grace busy as little is known about her early married years. As wife of the *Tanaist* to the clan she should have been able to watch closely many of the disputes and intrigues that her husband and the clan were involved in. One of Donal's most notorious deeds has been recorded in the Annals. The Annals of the Kingdom of Ireland are a written record of the times kept by the scribes known as the Four Masters.

The record relates how Donal was involved in the murder of Walter Fada Burke. Donal's sister Finola was Walter Fada's stepmother and it is believed that she planned the murder so that her own son Richard-an-Iarainn (Iron Richard) would become Chief of the Burkes. The murder was carried out at the O'Flaherty castle of Invernan. The Burkes were guests at the castle and as was the custom the men went off for the day hunting. As the hunting party was returning to the castle in the evening Walter Fada was attacked and hacked to death with an axe. Even in those bloodthirsty days the murder was considered shocking. It was much talked about among the great families of Connaught and because of his part in the foul deed Donal lost support among his own clan. Loss of support to someone hoping to be chief of the O'Flahertys was a serious matter. Under Gaelic law when a chieftain died his clan would gather to elect a new chieftain. His successor was chosen from among his family and was selected for his age and experience. A *Tanaist* would be elected at the same time. This system prevented the title passing to an infant son who could not defend it from other chieftains. This meant it was important for a *Tanaist* to have the support of the clan. Grace would have noticed this change in her husband's fortunes. She was quietly learning how power could be gained or lost.

During the early years of her marriage Grace impressed the O'Flaherty followers with her knowledge of seafaring. Whenever the clan gathered together in the great hall of Bunowen Castle to discuss matters of fishing, trading or piracy, Grace was always able to contribute with sound advice and sensible judgements. The time spent on the sea with her father during her childhood had not been wasted.

As time went on she got more and more involved in the seafaring activities of the clan. Eventually, by the time she was in her early twenties, she had gathered together a band of supporters from among her husband's followers and she started to lead expeditions herself.

The men must have been wary at first of being led by a woman but her expeditions were so successful and her courage and daring so impressive that before long they were ready to obey her every command.

SURRENDER AND REGRANT

Meanwhile Henry VIII, who became King of Ireland in 1541, had begun in earnest to implement the Tudor policy of extending the English Code of Law (Common Law) and the English language beyond the Pale. This policy was continued later by his children Edward VI and Elizabeth I. Slowly the English were making progress across the country. They succeeded in getting some of the Gaelic chieftains to submit to the Crown under the policy of Surrender and Regrant. This involved the chieftains surrendering their lands to the Crown and being regranted them with new English titles of Earl or Lord. They also had to swear an oath of allegiance to the Crown and promise to obey English law. Many submitted because they felt it was their best

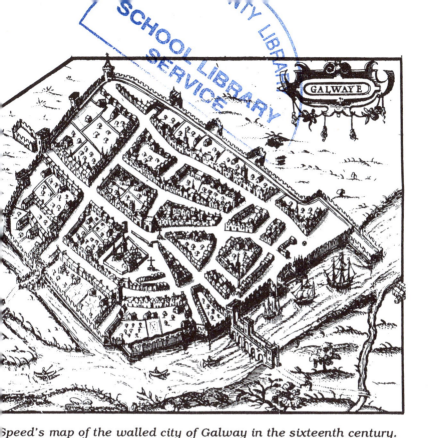

Speed's map of the walled city of Galway in the sixteenth century.

hope of keeping their lands. They had seen others who refused have their lands laid waste and their livestock confiscated. The Tudor conquest which was to change the face of Ireland was well under way.

However, the remoter parts of Connaught were largely untouched by English rule and many of the Gaelic chieftains in these areas were left alone and continued to live under the old Irish laws, known as the Brehon Laws. (These laws set out the rules

Sir Henry Sidney rides out of Dublin Castle to put down a rebellion.The heads of 'rebels' are displayed to warn others of what lies in store for them.

and regulations for living in Irish society.) Galway city was an exception. The inhabitants of Galway were descendants of Norman invaders who hadn't changed over to Irish ways and they continued to speak English and live according to English laws and customs. The city had for a long time been a great trading place. Galway had its own Charter and its corporation had passed many strict laws to keep unwanted traders out. Among them was a bye-law stating 'that neither O ne Mac (ie native Irish) shall strutte ne swagger thru the streets of Galway'. This was a very harsh rule and meant that the native Irish could not enter or trade in the city and was one of the reasons the O'Malleys traded abroad. However, these laws did not keep fearless Irish raiders out as an inscription carved over the west gate of the city by its inhabitants shows—'from the ferocious O'Flaherties, good Lord deliver me'.

Events did not move swiftly enough for Queen Elizabeth. She became very impatient with the Irish chieftains and their stubborn ways. Elizabeth wanted the whole country under English rule as the conquest was turning out to be a costly business to the Crown. She was losing money and some of her best soldiers in her efforts to gain control. So she pressed her newly appointed Lord Deputy, Sir Henry Sidney, to take action against those who would not obey.

In 1566, a year after his arrival in Ireland, Sidney sent for Ulick Burke, later to be granted the title the Earl of Clanrickard, and The McWilliam Iochtar as he feared they were about to join Shane O'Neill who was rebelling in the north. The two leaders came and submitted. Lord Deputy Sidney was delighted with his success and recorded that it was the first time that anyone holding the title of The MacWilliam Iochtar had ever submitted to the Crown. This act of submission by two of the great chieftains was a warning to the O'Malley and O'Flaherty clans that English rule was expanding beyond Galway into the territory of Iar-Connaught.

About this time a young O'Flaherty chief called Murrough-na-dTuadh (Murrough of the Battle-Axes), from a junior branch of the clan, was making a name for himself raiding his neighbours' lands and stealing their cattle. He was the cause of many skirmishes and great unrest. The English, fearing the unrest would spread, took a hand in the matter. In return for his submission they agreed to pardon Murrough for all past offences and furthermore to make him chieftain of the whole of Iar-Connaught, in other words The O'Flaherty. Under Brehon Law as a member of a junior branch of the clan he would not be considered for the chieftainship. The O'Flahertys of Iar-Connaught were outraged. At one stroke the English had deposed Donal Crone as chieftain and Donal-an-Chogaid as *Tanaist* and shattered the peace of Connaught.

Shortly after these events the first English Governor of Connaught was appointed. The Governor, Sir Edward Fitton, was described in his day as being an 'ill-tempered, quarrelsome man, not at all fitted for the delicate duty of turning Irish into English order'. He was a very bad choice and was hated by the Irish for his ruthless ways.

The Governor was not long in office when the Mayo Burkes, supported by Donal Crone and Donal-an-Chogaidh, rebelled. Fitton with the aid of the Earl of Clanrickard marched against them and a battle took place at Shrule. No-one knows who won the battle as both sides claimed victory, but because he had rebelled The MacWilliam was again forced to submit to the Crown. He was also made to pay a large sum in yearly rent to Queen Elizabeth. He died shortly afterwards. Little by little the Queen's men were subduing the Irish chieftains. The remaining chieftains now saw that they either had to band together, seek foreign help or submit to the crown. If they submitted they ran the risk of losing their hereditory rights, lands and privileges. Times were changing in Connaught.

SIEGE AT HEN'S CASTLE

About this time a great change was to take place in Grace's life. Her husband Donal had attacked and seized a Joyce clan fortress on Lough Corrib. When the Joyces tried to retake their fortress Donal

Terrified English soldiers flee Hen's Castle as Grace's
men pour molten metal down on them.

defended it so well they had to retreat. As a result of this victory he became know as Donal-an-Cullagh or Donal the Cock. The Joyces were furious and waited for an opportunity to take their revenge. Their chance came shortly afterwards when Donal went out hunting in the nearby mountains. There they ambushed and killed him. Luckily, some of Donal's followers who had survived the ambush rushed back to the castle to bring Grace the news of her Donal's death and to warn her of the Joyces' arrival. With great courage Grace rallied her men to defend the castle. When the Joyces arrived they expected to find the castle empty, and that Grace had fled. Instead Hen's Castle was occupied and fiercely defended. They attempted to mount an attack on the castle but were driven back. Finally they had to retreat leaving Grace in proud possession of the castle. The castle was ever afterwards known as Caislean-an-Circa, Hen's Castle, since Grace, as Donal the Cock's wife, had often been nicknamed the hen!

Some years later Grace was again besieged at Hen's Castle. She was there with only a few followers when a large force of English soldiers from Galway stormed the castle. Grace was determined not to surrender and be captured. All seemed lost. They had nothing further to defend themselves with. But Grace ordered her men to strip all the lead from the castle roof and melt it down. They wondered why until she ordered them to pour the molten metal over the turrets onto the attacking troops below. The soldiers made a hasty retreat to the safety of the mainland to regroup.

Still trapped in the castle she despatched one of her men, under cover of darkness, through an underground passage which connected the island to the mainland. He had orders to light a beacon on the nearby Hill of Doon. As part of her defence plan she had arranged that the lighted beacons on the coastline were to be a sign to her followers that she was in danger. Creeping up on the English from behind, her fleet took them by surprise, routed them and lifted the second siege of Hen's Castle. Grace O'Malley had a very narrow escape but her defence of the castle became a legend.

RETURN TO CLARE CASTLE

As the widow of a Gaelic chief Grace had the right to one-third of her husband's possessions but the O'Flaherty clan withheld this right from her. This made Grace and her family very dependent on the clan, a situation which she disliked. Gathering together her own band of supporters, including some of her late husband's followers, she set about earning her own living by trading both on land and at sea as her father had always done. In this way Grace became independent of the O'Flaherty clan.

Gaelic chiefs were not used to women in positions of power and the O'Flahertys were jealous of her success. They had not minded her previous activities at sea because then she had been operating as part of the O'Flaherty clan and her exploits added to the wealth and power of the O'Flahertys. Now, however, she was setting herself up as a leader and they feared she was becoming too powerful. To avoid a quarrel with the clan Grace decided to return home to her father's kingdom of Umhall Uachtarach. Owen Dubhdarra, her father, still ruled his kingdom and the O'Malley clan as an independent Gaelic chieftain. Unlike his neighbours

*When Grace returned home a widow, her father gave her
Clare Island Castle as her home.*

the Burkes and the O'Flahertys, he had not submitted to the English.

He was very proud of his only daughter,
welcomed her back and gave her the O'Malley castle
on Clare Island as her home. Her faithful band of

followers went with her. Grace was now a chieftain in her own right. She was responsible for providing a livelihood for the community she ruled over and for her band of fighting men who now numbered 200.

Clare Island Castle was a perfect stronghold for Grace. It was solidly built to withstand attack and cleverly positioned so that only those who knew the local waterways could navigate the dangerous passage to the entrance. There were windows or lookouts on all four sides of the castle. These gave a commanding view of the surrounding sea. Ships could be spotted a long distance away, giving Grace and her men ample time to launch their boats. When a ship likely to be laden with cargo was spotted, the boats would be launched and the unfortunate ship brought to a halt. Grace's men would swarm on board the ship while Grace carried on negotiations with the captain. The men would then wait for Grace's command. Sometimes she would order the ship to be completely stripped of its cargo. Other times she would make a bargain with the captain allowing him to go in peace if he handed over a certain amount of his cargo to her. The galleys would then speed back to the island laden with booty.

At that time piracy was a common practice among the seafaring clans on the west of Ireland and elsewhere. In England, Sir Walter Raleigh and Sir Francis Drake both became rich from piracy. With Galway closed to the native Irish, any ships, English or foreign, were considered fair targets for plunder and the clans grew rich on the booty.

Sir Walter Raleigh, who made his fortune and reputation in piracy. He was granted lands in Ireland in return for his services to the Crown.

Grace was the most successful and the most notorious pirate on the west coast. Her clever tactics and daring won her riches and success. Her tactics were the element of surprise and the speed with which she swooped on her target. The swiftness of her galleys was due to the skill and discipline of her oarsmen. Grace was very proud of the men under her command remarking that she would rather have a shipful of the Conroy and McAnnally clans than a shipful of gold.

Grace O'Malley loved the excitement, adventure and danger of the pirate's life though piracy was not her only source of income. The O'Malleys had for generations been great traders and Grace continued this tradition. Her fleet laden with cargoes of salted fish, hides, linen and woollens traded in Ulster, Scotland and, like her father, in Spain and Portugal. But it is for her activities as a pirate that she is famous. Her knowledge of the sea, her ability to lead, her courage plus the skill and bravery of her men made Granuaile the scourge of the western seaboard and a thorn in the side of the Galway merchants.

The mayor and corporation of Galway were furious at her behaviour. They complained to the English that the city's trade was being ruined by the O'Malleys. The English authorities noted the complaint and recorded many of Grace's illegal acts but they left her alone. They already had enough trouble on their hands trying to control the situation in Munster.

At this time Grace was becoming well-known, not only in her native province of Connaught, but throughout the whole of Ireland. The leading families in Ulster, the O'Neills and O'Donnells, often

This would have been the type of ship Grace met on her journeys to and from Spain.

employed her and her fleet of galleys to bring over fighting men, gallowglasses, from Scotland. Gallowglasses were like today's mercenaries. They fought for any cause in return for money. Wielding long broad axes, and wearing shirts of mail they fought on foot. They were ferocious fighters and hated to abandon any battlefield.

Thomas Butler, Earl of Ormond, also employed Grace and her galleys. It is thought that he was more interested in her smuggling activities and that she often brought in illegal cargoes for him from abroad. Through her seafaring activities she developed strong friendships with these people.

Later on in her life, in times of trouble, these friend-ships were to prove very important to her.

Grace is sometimes referred to as 'the Dark Lady of Doona'. There is a story that explains how she got that name. One winter's day after her return to Clare Island, Grace and her followers were making a pilgrimage to a Holy Well on the island. It was the first of February, St Brigid's Day, an important day at the time for praying and visiting holy places. It was a cold, stormy day with gale force winds blow-ing. While at the well news came that a foreign ship had been blown onto the rocks at Achill and was breaking up. In spite of the fierce gale Grace and her followers left their prayers and launched their boats into the stormy seas to salvage whatever cargo and riches the ship might have been carrying. When they reached the ship they encountered no opposition as all the crew appeared to have drowned. In jubilant mood they filled their boats with booty and were preparing to sail away when Grace noticed a young man, who seemed to be still alive, washed up on the rocks. She had him placed in her boat and took him back to her castle. There she nursed him slowly back to health. They spent a lot of time together and by the time he was fully recovered they had fallen in love.

Grace's new-found happiness was not to last however. While out hunting on the island one day the MacMahon clan spotted the stranger and attacked and killed him. The news was brought to Grace who, though grief-stricken, immediately set out to take revenge on the killers. She found the MacMahon boats pulled up on the island of Cahir. She landed on the island, destroyed their boats and killed the men responsible for the death of her loved one. She then sailed for the MacMahon castle of Doona in Blacksod Bay. She attacked the castle, drove out the inhabitants and installed her own followers in it. The name, the Dark Lady of Doona, was given to Grace in memory of these events.

SECOND MARRIAGE

Richard-an-Iarainn (Iron Richard Burke) who was now *Tanaist* to the MacWilliam title, just as his mother Finola had planned, owned and lived in the next territory to the O'Malleys. He was a wealthy man with a large army of gallowglasses in his pay. He also had his own fleet and one day would be The MacWilliam Iochtair. A banding together of these two powerful families would make them a force against the invading English. No doubt Richard and Grace saw these advantages for in due course they married. She is said to have married him for 'one year certain'. This meant that should either one of them wish to opt out of the marriage they could do so after one year. Brehon laws allowed for divorce by both men and woman in a marriage contract.

Rockfleet now became home to Grace and her followers. There is a tradition which says that a year after the wedding Grace O'Malley stood on the castle battlements and shouted down to Richard 'I dismiss you', thus ending the marriage. This is only a story however. What probably happened was that one day, when the year had ended Richard had returned from an expedition to find the castle locked against him. Grace then appeared on the battlements and shouted down to him a list of the terms on which she was prepared to continue the marriage. He must have been happy to accept these terms because they remained husband and wife

Rockfleet, which became Grace's home when she married Richard-an-Iarainn.

until Richard's death.

Richard and Grace had one son who was known as Tibbot-na-Long or Theobald of the Ships. It is said that Tibbot was born to Grace on board ship when she was returning from a trading mission.

According to the story, the day after his birth, while Grace was resting below deck, the ship was attacked by Turkish pirates. A fierce battle ensued. The Turks were winning when the captain ran below and begged Grace to come up and rally the men. She rushed up shouting at her men to fight harder. Firing a blunderbuss she blasted the Turks off their feet. Inspired by her fighting spirit the men fought with renewed vigour and finally won the day. Another heroic tale was added to the legend of Granuaile.

ROCKFLEET

Grace spent many years at Rockfleet and became more and more involved in the power struggles and intrigues of the clan. The castle still stands to this day. It is four storeys high with extremely thick stone walls. The castle was designed to withstand a siege. The living quarters, which were on the fourth floor, could be completely cut off from the rest of the castle and even had fire-proof flooring. There was always a worry that the enemy would set fire to the castle. A doorway on the east wall of the living area leads out and down to the rocks some 50 feet below. The door probably had a twofold use, firstly as an escape exit by lowering ropes, and secondly as a loading bay. Sacks of provisions, heavy furniture or arms could be hoisted from below by means of a pulley. The castle also has an early stone privy with a pit out to the tide. The living area was very comfortable with a large fireplace with seats on either side. There is one large and several small windows to give light and on one wall a loop-hole slit. Legend has it that Grace had a rope running from her favourite ship through the slit and tied to her toe at night! In the event of an attack or attempted theft any tug on the rope acted as a warning signal.

HOSTAGE

Grace's son Tibbot-na-Long spent his early childhood at Rockfleet where, like his mother, he learned to love boats and the sea. Later as a youth he went as a hostage to the Bingham household in England. This stay in England is known from a letter written by Queen Elizabeth I to Sir Richard Bingham. In it the Queen refers to Grace's 'second son Tibbot Burk, one that hath been brought up civilly with your brother and can speak English'. At some stage Tibbot must have been given as a hostage in order to guarantee either Grace or Richard's good behaviour. Giving a son as a hostage was common practice at the time in Ireland. The boys were sent to be brought up with English families. The idea was that they would learn the English language and customs and on returning to their clans would be obedient to the English Crown and its laws.

It must have been a hard blow for Grace to have to hand over her young son to the Binghams. Having her son brought up away from home would not have bothered her too much, because fosterage was a common practice in Ireland. This involved children from one family being sent to a different family to be reared. It was a very effective means of strengthening alliances between families. It was a different matter, however, for Grace to have to send her son far away to a strange and hostile country where the language, the customs and the whole way of life were different.

Attacked by Turkish pirates, the story goes that Grace rushed on deck and blasted them off the ship.

Trouble continued to break out in Ireland from time to time. In Connaught, Sir Edward Fitton ruled the province with an iron hand. He was ruthless with anyone who showed the least sign of rebelling. However, undeterred, Grace continued to attack and plunder the ships heading for Galway. The merchants were furious and complained bitterly to Fitton. Eventually he was forced to act against her.

Fitton chose Captain William Martin to lead the English force sent out to put a stop to Grace's illegal activities. On 8 March 1574, the force of both ships and troops sailed out of Galway harbour. They took Grace by complete surprise and she was trapped in Rockfleet. Captain Martin and his men laid siege to the castle. Once again Grace O'Malley's pluck inspired her men to stand fast and on the eighteenth day she turned the tide of battle into an attack. Captain Martin and his troops fled, glad to escape capture. It was a great victory for Grace.

CHIEFTAINS SUBMIT TO SIDNEY

England's Lord Deputy in Ireland, Sir Henry Sidney, visited Galway in March 1576. While there he ordered the submission of all the chieftains and lords of Connaught. They were slow to come to Galway which had long been a hostile city to the native Irish. However, The MacWilliam Iochtar, Shane MacOliverus, did come to the city and duly promised obedience to the Crown. This was a continuation of the policy of Surrender and Regrant but in addition The MacWilliam also promised to accept 'cess'.

'Cess' was a promise to provide food and lodging for the soldiers of the English army for part of the year. The length of the stay depended on the army's

Portrait of Lord Deputy Sir Henry Sidney.

needs. From now on The MacWilliam would have to
provide for 200 soldiers and their horses for two
months every year. Sidney wrote that he found The
MacWilliam a very sensible and civil person who,
though he could speak no English, could converse
in Latin. In return for his submission the Lord

Deputy gave Shane MacOliverus a knighthood and 'some other little Trifles'.

Several other Irish chieftains followed The Mac-William's example and submitted. For the first time that we know of The O'Malley submitted. Sidney recorded that he was 'an originall Irishe man, strong in galleys and Seamen' and that he promised to obey the Queen and 'to pay her Rent and Service'. The O'Malley who made the submission was not Grace's father Owen Dubhdarra who had died but Melaghlin O'Malley who had succeeded him as chief. With this submission the ancient Irish order in the O'Malley territory came to an end.

The Lord Deputy returned to Dublin well satisfied. All the most important chieftains had come to Galway and submitted. This may have been partly due to the arrival in Connaught of Sir Nicholas Malby who had been appointed to take over from Fitton. He was much more reasonable to deal with than Fitton.

On a subsequent visit to Galway by the Lord Deputy Sidney, Grace and her husband Richard-an-Iarainn came of their own accord to meet him. As power now rested with the English, Grace, with her keen sense of survival, decided it was better to be on good terms with them.

Sir Henry Sidney writing about the occasion noted that she came to offer her services 'wheresoever I would command Her'. He described Grace as the most 'notorious woman in all the coasts of Ireland'. He also noted that she had 'a most feminine' appearance.

The Lord Deputy's son Philip Sidney, who was a well-known poet and courtier at Queen Elizabeth's court, was delighted by Grace and talked to her for

Grace and Richard-an-Iarainn meet Sir Henry Sidney in Galway. On this occasion they came to offer their services but not to submit.

a long time. Perhaps among other things they talked about Hugh O'Neill whom they both knew well. Hugh O'Neill was a member of the ruling family in Ulster, the Earls of Tyrone. Nearly 20 years previously, in 1559, he had been taken from Ulster, at the age of nine, by Philip's father and had been reared and educated with Philip in their home in England. Sir Henry hoped that this English education would ensure that O'Neill would remain loyal to the Crown on his return to Ulster.

After offering her services to the Lord Deputy Grace returned home to live as she had always done — trading and raiding on land and on sea. She is said to have subdued most of the county of Mayo and to have rampaged and rustled cattle from Donegal to Waterford.

HOWTH CASTLE

One of Grace O'Malleys most famous exploits is said to have taken place around this time. While returning from a trading expedition, Grace landed at Howth. She went to the castle there in search of hospitality. It was a Gaelic custom for one chief to give hospitality to another friendly chief if he was passing through his territory. Legend relates that Grace found the gates of the castle locked and she was not allowed in as the lord was dining and did not wish to be disturbed. She was raging at this slight and, still furious, returned to her ship in the nearby harbour. Meeting the young heir to the castle playing down by the sea she seized him, put him on board her ship and set sail for home.

The young boy's father went to Connaught and pleaded with Grace for his son's safe return at any price. But Grace O'Malley was not interested in

43

money in return for the insult she had suffered and demanded instead a promise that the gates of Howth Castle would never again be closed to anyone looking for hospitality and that an extra plate would always be laid at the dinner table. The Lord of Howth Castle readily agreed to this simple request as he had greatly feared that the notorious Granuaile would demand much more. To this day the Gainsfort-St Lawrence family still set an extra place at the dinner table in Howth Castle!

IMPRISONMENT

In 1577 while raiding the Earl of Desmond's lands in the south of the country Grace was captured by the Earl and imprisoned in Limerick gaol for a year and half. Desmond, who was being watched closely by the English as his loyalty to the Crown was suspect, handed Grace over to Lord Justice Drury, the President of Munster, to prove he was a faithful servant of the Queen. Drury wrote to the Lord Deputy in Dublin with the news of Grace's capture. He described her as 'a great spoiler and chief commander and director of thieves and murderers at sea to spoille this province'. Some months later, perhaps after he got to know her, he wrote of Grace again, this time more kindly, saying that she was famous for her courage and her exploits at sea and that he was sending her to Dublin.

On arrival in Dublin Grace was put in the dungeons of Dublin Castle. They were rat-infested places, dark, airless and damp with water running down the walls. She hated being imprisoned in the unhealthy place after her active life outdoors and on the sea. Time dragged on and Grace saw many of those captured with her sent to the gallows. But

Imprisoned in the dungeons of Dublin Castle, Grace must have longed to be home in Connaught.

again she was lucky and was finally released in 1579 on condition that she gave up her pirating career. We can only guess that in order to get back to Connaught she agreed to this condition. Once again Grace O'Malley had survived and her legend grew.

THE DESMOND REBELLION

That summer Ireland was full of rumours of yet another rebellion. These rumours were to prove true. In July 1579 Sir James Fitzmaurice also known as 'Captain of Desmond' landed at Smerwick in County Kerry with a force of about 700 men. Sir James had been given money and troops by the King of Spain, Philip II, and Pope Gregory, in order to overthrow the 'heritic Queen' (Elizabeth) and drive her army from Ireland. Sir James begged help from the Gaelic chieftains including his cousin Gerald, Earl of Desmond, the man who had captured Grace O'Malley. Gerald refused to assist. In order to seek further support Sir James set out for Limerick where he was discovered and shot dead. Sir John of Desmond, the Earl's brother, on hearing the news took over as leader of the revolt. When news of Sir James' death reached Gerald he decided it was time to show his true colours and he joined the rebels.

The Earl of Desmond now urged The MacWilliam and Grace's husband Richard-an-Iarainn to support the uprising. The MacWilliam refused but Richard did not hesitate. He was joined by the Clandonnells, the O'Malleys, Ulick Burke and some of the O'Flahertys. With this army Richard plundered the neighbouring territories.

Sir Nicholas Malby, who had been sent over from

England to take charge of Connaught, set out against Richard and his forces. He was determined to put down the revolt. Malby was an experienced soldier and by clever tactics he lured the Clandonnells, who were gallowglasses and Richard's best fighting men, away from their leader. With these out of the way Malby then defeated Richard's right-hand man, Shane McHubert, took his castle Conamona and in a fit of merciless revenge killed everyone in it, men, women and children. Richard and what was left of his followers fled to the islands. The Desmond rebellion was short-lived in Connaught.

Malby, happy with his victory, retired to Ballyknock where on 16 February 1580 'Grany ni Maille and certain of her kinsmen came to me'. With Richard defeated, Grace, once again making the best of a bad situation, came to Malby and submitted. This way she could save some of her lands even if the rebellious Richard were taken.

Next Malby went to Burrishoole, near Newport, to inspect the lands owned by Richard-an-Iarainn, He was surprised by what he saw. Great stocks of timber and marble, good land and excellent fishing. He obviously did not expect the wild Irish chieftains to live so well as he noted all in a dispatch. He noted too the plentiful iron mines. Many believe that it was from these mines that Richard got his nickname. From these notes, which still exist, we know that Richard-an-Iarainn and Grace O'Malley were surrounded by plenty and lived very prosperously from the profits of their trade in wool, marble, salted fish and even iron.

When Malby departed Grace probably advised Richard that the time had come to submit, for very

*Burrishoole
Abbey,
in the territory
of the Burkes.*

shortly afterwards he went to Galway where he gave his pledge and was allowed to return home. As far as we know his only loss was the tribute money from the English fishing fleet which Malby had stopped till 'Her Majesty's pleasure be known'. He was lucky that his lands were not taken. The revolt was over in Connaught, though the Desmonds would fight on in Munster for another three years.

In November of this eventful year The MacWilliam died. Shane MacOliverus had been a peaceful chief. The same could not be said of his successor, Grace's husband Richard-an-Iarainn. Richard, though knighted by the English, continued his turbulent ways. He avoided the English and confined himself to fighting other clansmen. No doubt Grace, who was now enjoying her role as a great chieftain's wife, saw to it that Richard did not upset the Crown forces.

When Malby invited all the heads of the Gaelic clans in the west to a meeting in Galway he noted that Grace was among the wives present and that she 'thinketh herself to be no small lady ...'. Again she made an impression as she is the only wife mentioned in Malby's dispatch. For the remaining years of Richard's reign Mayo, the territory of the Burkes, was quiet and despite his warring life he died a natural death. The Four Masters recorded Richard's death noting that he was 'a plundering warlike unquiet and rebellious man.'

Grace was now a widow for the second time in her life. As Richard's widow she was entitled by Irish law to one-third of his possessions. From her experience with the O'Flahertys after Donal-an-Chogaidh'ssdeath, she had learned that the rights of widows were often ignored. This time she decided not to wait to be given her rights. For some time before Richard's death they had been living away from Rockfleet. Now, immediately her husband died, Grace gathered together all her followers, her 1,000 head of cattle and marched to Rockfleet where she installed herself. With her fierce reputation on land and sea she knew nobody would dare try to dislodge her.

In the same year, 1583, the Desmond rebellion in Munster finally came to an end. Throughout the year the rebel chieftains had been surrendering one after another. The Earl of Desmond himself refused to surrender and went into hiding in the mountains in Kerry. It was here that he was finally captured and killed in November of 1583. On his death all his vast land holdings throughout Munster were confiscated by the English authorities. They were then shared out among English settlers. The Queen's favourite at the time, Sir Walter Raleigh, was given the largest estate of all, 42,000 acres between Youghal and Lismore. It was on these lands that Raleigh grew the first potatoes ever planted in Ireland. Within 50 years they were to become the principal food in the Irish diet.

THE BINGHAM BROTHERS

A year later, in 1584, Sir Nicholas Malby died and is mentioned in the Annals as having been a fair ruler though 'he placed all Connaught under bondage'. Queen Elizabeth appointed Sir Richard Bingham to be the new Governor. Bingham was a much more ruthless man. He showed little mercy to anyone who went against the English laws. During a Burke rebellion Sir Richard had a member of the clan and his two sons hanged though none of the three had been involved in the fighting. His cruel and unjust ways even led the new Lord Deputy, Sir John Perrott, to give protection to some of the rebels.

When unrest continued in the province Bingham sent his brother, Captain John Bingham, into Grace O'Malley's territory to arrest her. After the arrest Grace and her followers were tied with rope and brought to Galway city. The Governor had a new gallows made from which to hang Grace. She thought her end had come and that she would find no escape this time. The night dragged on and all seemed lost. Grace had decided to face the gallows with her head held high; she would show Bingham

Lady Raleigh, wife of Sir Walter who was granted a huge estate near Youghal, Co. Cork.

she had no fear of death. But her luck held true as always and at the last minute she was set free when Richard Burke, her son-in-law (whose nickname was the Devil's Hook) promised that he would give himself up as a hostage if Grace continued disobeying British authority. This was a very gallant act on his part. In return for her freedom Grace had to pledge good conduct.

Grace may have escaped with her life but Bingham was determined to punish her so he confiscated her herds, over 1,000 cattle and horses in all. Worse was to follow.

At the end of the Burke rebellion Captain Bingham entered the territory of Owen O'Flaherty, Grace's eldest son. Although Owen was married to a Burke he had taken no part in the revolt but that did not deter Captain Bingham from inflicting further punishment. He rounded up 4,000 cattle, 100 sheep and nearly 500 horses — all the clan's livestock. Bingham claimed they were taken to pay for the expenses incurred by the British army during the rebellion. Still not satisfied he hanged 18 of Owen's followers and while the O'Flaherty clan were mourning their dead he connived to have Owen murdered on the pretext that he was trying to escape.

This was the worst time in Grace O'Malley's long and eventful life. Bingham had taken her herds, had murdered her eldest son, confiscated all his family's livestock and left the clans destitute. In the face of such terror Richard Burke, the Devil's Hook, rebelled. Grace, knowing that the Binghams would arrest her next, fled by sea to her friends The O'Neill and The O'Donnell in Ulster. Even on her journey north her troubles continued. She ran into a terrible storm and her ships were wrecked. O'Neill and O'Donnell welcomed Grace with true Gaelic hospitality and she remained in Ulster for three months.

We can imagine that Grace would have got on

particularly well with the O'Donnell chieftain's wife, Inion Dubh. Like Grace she was a strong, dominant woman and a leader in her own right. This is one description we have of her: 'though she was calm and deliberate and much praised for her womanly qualities, she had the heart of a hero and the mind of a soldier. She had many troops from Scotland and some of the Irish at her disposal and under her control and in her own time and pay constantly.' Inion and Grace must have had many stories to swap during Grace's long stay in Donegal.

While she was there news reached her that Sir Richard Bingham had been ordered by Queen Elizabeth to serve in her army in Flanders. With Bingham's departure in July, 1587, Grace returned to Rockfleet Castle to rebuild her fleet and resume her life at sea. With all her herds taken this was now her only means of livelihood.

A few months after her return Grace learned of a disgraceful act of treachery by Lord Deputy Perrott who had been appointed to Ireland. Red Hugh O'Donnell, the chieftain's son, and a party of friends had been invited to entertainment on board a ship rented by Perrott. The ship laden with wine was anchored in Lough Swilly as the Lord Deputy knew Red Hugh was staying with friends nearby. Red Hugh and his party went on board and wine was served in the captain's cabin. While the guests were drinking below deck the ship set sail for Dublin, kidnapping the whole party. Young Red Hugh was imprisoned in Dublin Castle for the next three years. He escaped but was recaptured and as a further punishment he was put in irons. A year later, on Christmas night, he escaped again but the weather was terrible and he was trapped in snow in the Wicklow mountains. Both his feet were frozen and he had to have his big toes cut off because they were so badly frostbitten. It was only after a long and painful journey that he reached the north.

The capture of her friend Red Hugh and his imprisonment in Dublin Castle and above all the sorry plight of the O'Malley and O'Flaherty clans led Grace to seek a pardon from Queen Elizabeth. This was duly granted on the 4 May 1588. Grace timed this pardon well for very shortly afterwards her old enemy Sir Richard Bingham returned to Connaught as Governor.

THE ARMADA

Rumours of a great Spanish fleet gathering to fight the English first reached Grace during her stay in Ulster. As the rumours spread throughout the country the English Government made it a crime to aid any Spanish invasion force that landed in Ireland. The penalty for anyone caught helping the Spanish was death.

The great Armada set sail from the port of Corunna in July 1588. They sailed in a half-moon, or crescent, formation which the Spanish commanders believed would make the fleet unbeatable. On 30 July the Armada reached the English Channel. For a week the Spanish fought the English fleet led by Lord Howard and Sir Francis Drake. Day and night the battle raged. The Spanish galleons were unable to keep their formation during the battle. The enormous galleons, the pride of the Spanish fleet, proved awkward in battle. Their very size, which had been thought to be their strength, made them slow to manoeuvre. This meant that the smaller, fast-moving English warships were able to

The Spanish fleet in the crescent formation which they wrongly thought would make them unbeatable.

attack and out-gun the Spaniards. The use of fire-ships, small boats packed with wood, straw and gunpowder was another tactic used by the English. The fireships were set alight and directed towards the huge galleons from close quarters causing fear and panic. Then the weather suddenly changed and the Spanish fleet, with no safe port to retreat to, scattered. The battle was over.

Some of the Spanish ships tried to sail around Scotland and Ireland and reach Spain by the round-about route. This they felt was their best chance as the English held the Channel route to Europe. The Armada suffered greater losses on the treacherous

The launch of the English fire ships.

Scottish and Irish coasts than in battle. Their mighty galleons were dashed against the rocks by fierce gales and broke up; others sank in the terrible Atlantic storms that raged. Many drowned and some of those who did scramble ashore fared little better.

Eye witness accounts tell of seeing as many as 1,100 corpses lying on the strand at Streedagh in Sligo. The miserable survivors got a mixed reception from the Irish. Some Gaelic chiefs gave them shelter but others stripped the Spaniards naked and left them to their fate. Many were caught, tortured and hanged by the English who were guarding the coast. Greed for the treasures said to be on

Spanish galleons.

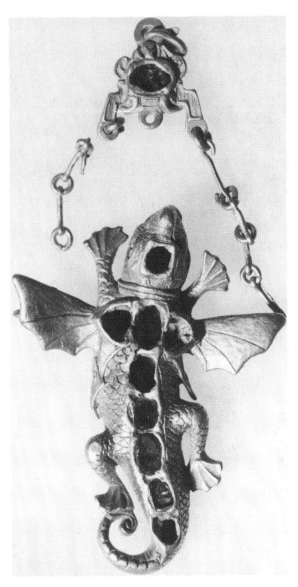

Salamander pendant from the Spanish Armada ships which sank off the Irish coast.

sixteenth-century cannon. Both English and Spanish had cannons mounted on their warships.

A food vessel, from the Spanish Armada.

board the ships and the fear of being hanged if caught aiding the unfortunate Spaniards may have caused some to act as they did.

The *Rata*, one of the finest of the galleons, foundered in Blacksod Bay where Richard Burke, a grandson of Grace O'Malley, robbed and mistreated the survivors. When O'Rourke, Prince of Breffni, heard of this outrage he sent assistance to the Spaniards. He invited Commander De Layva and his men to his castle at Dromahair. For this act of mercy he was later hanged.

Whether Grace O'Malley helped or hindered the Spanish we do not know but some of her kinsmen are known to have killed nearly 300 men from the ship of Don Pedro de Mendoza which had foundered on Clare Island. The Spanish captain, not knowing whether the locals were Irish or English, friendly or hostile, refused to surrender and the O'Malleys slaughtered every one.

Most of the ships that set out with the Armada did return home to Spain but between the battle and the gales there was great loss of life with severe damage to the fleet.

BURKE REBELLION

Sir Richard Bingham was furious that some of the Irish chiefs in his territory had sheltered the Spaniards and refused to hand them over to the English authorities. On his orders anybody who had helped the Spaniards was hunted down and imprisoned or hanged. This harsh treatment caused great resentment among the Irish.

Early in 1589 Bingham was away in Ulster with his troops and the Irish chieftains in Connaught took advantage of his absence to stage a rebellion.

An angry Grace sets out for Bunowen to take revenge on her son who had supported Bingham against her.

The main leaders of the rebellion were Grace's son-in-law, the Devil's Hook, her son Tibbot, who had recently been released, Murrough of the Battle-Axes, who had always sided with the Queen's forces until now, and Robert O'Malley. Grace, who was now nearly 60, helped the rebellion by ferrying fighting men in her galleys to wherever they were needed.

The rebellion went from strength to strength during the year and in October the Burkes elected a new chieftain to rule over them in the old Irish way. The election of old style Irish chieftains had for a long time been forbidden by the English. There was little that Richard Bingham could do about the rebellion since he himself was on trial in Dublin at the time. He had made himself unpopular with both the English and the Irish and was facing charges brought against him by both sides.

In December, however, the charges were dismissed and he came back to Connaught in January, 1590. He immediately got together an army and set about putting down the rebellion. He attacked the castle of the Burkes, killed the inhabitants and destroyed their lands. By the end of the month the rebellion was over. The Burkes and their allies agreed to peace terms.

Grace, not knowing that the rebellion was over, set off with three boats and attacked and plundered property belonging to an Englishman, Sir Thomas La Strange. When Bingham heard about this he would have marched into Grace's territory to arrest her had not Richard Burke the Devil's Hook again interceded on her behalf. He promised she would repair the damage and restore the property stolen and offered himself as hostage if she did not. So once again, Grace narrowly escaped falling into Bingham's clutches.

As far as Grace was concerned, however, before this rebellion was well and truly over with she had one more job to do. Her son, Murrough O'Flaherty, had fought on Bingham's side in the rebellion.

Grace was outraged that her own son should have aided her arch-enemy Bingham against her. So she got her galleys together and sailed off to her old home of Bunowen which was now the home of her son.

On landing there she killed three or four men who came out to oppose her. After filling her boats with cattle and other goods she had plundered she sailed back home again satisfied with the revenge she had taken on her son.

In spite of her age, her life at sea was as active as ever. In June of the same year, Scots mercenaries came down from Ulster and sailed into Burke territory where they killed some of Grace's relations and made off with their property. On hearing of this Grace got together 20 galleys and set off in hot pursuit after them. This event is described in a letter Bingham wrote to the Lord Deputy. In the letter he says he didn't interfere because he was hoping both parties might kill each other off in the fight, thus freeing him of trouble-makers, 'which I am contented to tollerate, hoping that all or the moste parte will take their journey towardes heaven and the province ridd of manie badd and ill disposed persons'.

Times were changing in Connaught, however, and more and more territory was coming under Bingham's control. The days when Grace could rule the seas from her castle at Rockfleet were over. The coastline where once she had lain in wait with her galleys to pounce on unwary boats was now patrolled by English ships. She could no longer sail out of her hidden inlets to demand payment in return for free passage or to plunder ships carrying rich cargoes. Her income from her seafaring activities was thus greatly reduced and her income from her land had never fully recovered since John Bingham had seized her cattle four years earlier in 1587.

It suited Bingham and the English administrators in Ireland to have Grace and the Burkes deprived of power and wealth at this time. In the early 1590s the English were getting more and more nervous about the situation in Ulster where Hugh O'Neill held power. O'Neill had returned to Ireland in 1566, having been brought up for seven years in the home of Sir Henry Sidney. On his return home O'Neill set about making himself the most powerful man in Ulster. At first he appeared to be loyal to the English Crown and in 1585 he was given the title Earl of Tyrone by the Queen. However, as time went by the English began to suspect him of plotting with the Spanish to overthrow English rule in Ireland. When young Red Hugh O'Donnell made his daring escape from Dublin Castle in 1592 they suspected O'Neill had organised it but they could not prove anything.

Bingham knew about Grace's close friendship with O'Neill and the O'Donnells and he was determined to limit her activities so he could keep a close eye on her. He was afraid that if there was trouble in Ulster she would go to help her friends. In a letter he wrote about this time he refers to her as 'a notable traitoress and nurse to all rebellions in the Province for 40 years'.

Queen Elizabeth I
in all her splendour.

GRACE IN LONDON

Grace was not prepared to live out her life in poverty, so in 1593 she wrote to Queen Elizabeth looking for help. During that year both her brother, Donal-na-Piopa, and her son, Tibbot, were arrested and thrown in prison. When this happened she decided that writing letters was not enough and she made plans to go to London in person to look for help for herself and release from prison for her brother and son.

In late July she set sail. Sailing and piloting one of her own ships from the west of Ireland to London would have posed no problems for Grace. The main danger lay in avoiding English patrol boats. We can imagine what a prize prisoner this famous pirate queen would have been to an English sea-captain! No-one would have believed her story of going to London on a peaceful mission to ask for an audience with the Queen. She managed however to evade patrols and she arrived safely London.

London at that time was a thriving, bustling city of about 200,000 people. Not a big city in modern terms but at that time it was one of the biggest cities in Europe. It was a city of hovels for the poor and magnificent palaces for the rich.

We can only guess at the reasons why Queen Elizabeth agreed to a meeting with Grace. Elizabeth was at this time ruler of one of the most powerful countries in the world and there would have been many demands on her time. Perhaps she was curious to see this famous sea-queen she had heard so much about in letters from Bingham, Sidney and others. She probably felt she had a lot in common with Grace. They were both about the same age and had lived most unusual lives for women, being strong rulers and leaders of men. She might also have been persuaded to grant the audience by Grace's old friend, Black Tom, the Earl of Ormond, who was one of Elizabeth's closest friends at court.

The meeting of these two legendary women took place in Greenwich Castle just outside London. Although no record of the meeting survives we can still picture the scene: Elizabeth, who had a passion for clothes, magnificent in a many-layered, jewel-encrusted gown; Grace, in the simple linen tunic and cloak of an Irish noble woman. We can be sure the fine ladies and gentlemen of the court must have jostled each other for a view of the Irish pirate and chieftain.

The meeting between Grace and Queen Elizabeth at Greenwich Castle, London.

67

An old song describes Grace in court:

That sun-burnt brow did fearless thoughts reveal;
And in her girdle was a skeyne of steel;
Her crimson mantle, a gold brooch did bind;
Her flowing garments reached unto her heel;
Her hair-part fell in tresses unconfined,
And part, a silver bodkin did fasten up behind.

There is one story that has come down to us about the famous meeting. It is said that during the interview one of the ladies-in-waiting, seeing Grace needed a handkerchief, offered her a dainty one of linen and lace. After using it Grace threw it into the fire. When she was told she should have put it in her pocket she replied that the Irish had a higher standard of cleanliness as they would never keep a soiled article.

The interview was conducted in Latin. This was the language usually used by the Irish chieftains to communicate with the English since most of them had no English, and the English spoke no Irish. Grace explained away her illegal activities over the past 40 years by saying that, due to the constant warfare in Connaught, she had had to take to arms to defend herself and her property. She then went on to ask the Queen to order Bingham to grant her her rightful inheritance from both her husbands' properties. She requested permission from the Queen to be allowed 'to invade with sword and fire all your highness's enemies, wheresoever they are or shall without any interruption of any person or persons whatsoever'. The 'person' referred to here is Bingham and what she was really looking for was permission to carry on unhindered her raiding and plundering activities under the pretence of fighting against the Queen's enemies. She then turned her attention to the needs of her family and requested that Tibbot and Donal-na-Piopa be released from prison and that her son, Murrough, as a loyal subject of the Queen, be left in complete control of all her lands and property.

Grace must have made a great impression on Elizabeth because after the meeting the Queen wrote to Bingham ordering him to grant Grace's requests. We can imagine how annoyed Bingham must have been to get this letter since he had spent a lot of time during the previous seven years trying to curtail her activities.

Grace had taken a great risk presenting herself at court, the very heart of the English system of administration and justice. With her long record of involvement in piracy and rebellion she could have been thrown into the Tower of London, like many an Irish leader before her, and might never have seen Ireland again. Her daring paid off, however, and she went home well satisfied with her mission.

On her return she contacted Bingham immediately to demand that he carry out the Queen's orders. Her high hopes of a speedy return to her former lifestyle were soon dashed however. After repeated messages from Grace, Bingham reluctantly released Tibbot and Donal but he was determined not to allow Grace resume her old position of power and wealth.

O'NEILL AND THE ULSTER REBELLION

Bingham at this time had his hands full trying to keep the situation in Ulster under control. Attacks on English settlers and English military forts in the province were becoming more and more frequent and Bingham suspected O'Neill of building up forces in preparation for a rebellion. Therefore when Grace started building up her sea fleet again he immediately took measures to stop her. He sent a number of soldiers to live with her and her followers and he sent a Captain Strittas and a company of soldiers with orders that they accompany her on every voyage. The cost of feeding the soldiers and their animals soon rendered her almost penniless and the surveillance of Captain Strittas and his men meant she couldn't recoup any income from piracy or smuggling at sea.

By the end of 1594 she was in such desperation that one night, under cover of darkness, she slipped away in her boats with her followers and sailed to Munster to seek help from her friend Thomas Butler, Earl of Ormond. He received her kindly and wrote to the Lord Treasurer explaining her situation and asking that her request for the removal of the soldiers from her territory be granted. There was no reply to this petition however because by this time, 1595, the English administration in Dublin was fully occupied trying to cope with the growing unrest in Ulster.

In February 1595 O'Neill for the first time sided openly with the Irish rebels. With his forces he attacked a company of soldiers who had come with reinforcements and essential supplies for the English fort in Monaghan. Many English soldiers were killed in this battle which came to be called the Battle of Clontibret. Events moved very rapidly after this. Other English forts fell to the rebels and in June 1595 O'Donnell marched into Connaught from Donegal overcoming any English resistance on the way. When news of this reached Grace she returned home with her followers to welcome O'Donnell into Mayo.

Once again Grace's hopes were high. Her friends O'Neill and O'Donnell now controlled most of Ulster and Connaught and as an added bonus her old enemy Bingham had fled to England.

In December 1595 O'Donnell announced that the Burkes should have a chieftain again as in the old days. He named a day and invited all the chieftains of Mayo to come for the inauguration of the new chieftain, the next The MacWilliam. We can imagine the atmosphere of confidence and pride at this gathering of the clans of Mayo. It had been a long time since they had been able to gather together like this in accordance with the old traditions.

Grace was there with her followers and in view of her long friendship with O'Donnell she was hoping that her son Tibbot would be named as the new chieftain. Disappointment lay in store for her again. The title went to a son of another supporter of O'Donnell. O'Donnell made a mistake in overlooking Tibbot's claims to the leadership of the Burkes, for as a result he lost both Tibbot's and Grace's friendship and support. For the rest of O'Neill's and O'Donnell's campaign against Elizabeth's forces Tibbot fought on the side of the English. The loss of Tibbot's expert seamanship was a blow to O'Donnell's campaign in Connaught.

By this time, the land of Connaught was devastated as a result of constant warfare. Most of the cattle had been taken to feed O'Donnell's army and the crops had been destroyed. The clans were divided in their loyalties, some fighting with O'Neill and O'Donnell, some fighting with the English.

Tibbot, to prove his loyalty to Elizabeth and to gain free pardons and privileges for himself and Grace and other members of the family, had given his son Myles as a hostage to live in an English household as he himself had done in his youth.

Although Grace was now in her mid-60s, she was still active at sea. Records from these years mention her galleys being involved in various raids and skirmishes.

The rebellion was now in its fourth year and gathering momentum all the time. On 14 August 1598, O'Neill and O'Donnell won a major victory over the English at the Battle of the Yellow Ford. This victory was a great morale boost to the Irish cause and the rebellion spread into the midlands and the south. The settlers, who had taken land in Munster after the defeat of the Earl of Desmond in 1583, were attacked, their cattle raided and their houses burned to the ground. Most of the settlers left their lands and fled into the fortified towns.

For the next two years O'Neill went from strength to strength, extending his control over the country. He had been promised help from Spain and he eagerly awaited news of the arrival of a Spanish expedition. With the assistance of the Spaniards he confidently expected to overthrow English rule in Ireland once and for all and to install himself as the ruler of Ireland.

Grace was now about 70 and around this time she must have retired from seafaring to spend her last few years at Rockfleet. The last time her name appears in the records is in a dispatch, dated 1601, sent by an English captain patrolling the sea off the western coast. He mentions intercepting one of Grace's galleys which was on its way to plunder

MacSweeney territory in Donegal. She was not on board the galley herself but was still probably directing the fleet from her castle.

The tide began to turn against O'Neill at the beginning of 1601 with the appointment of a ruthless soldier, Lord Mountjoy, as Governor of Ireland. With a relentless campaign of fire and sword he managed to drive the rebels out of Munster and Leinster.

Now the need for help from Spain became more urgent. At last, towards the end of the year 1601 the news O'Neill and O'Donnell had been waiting for finally arrived. The Spaniards had landed — but in the wrong place. They landed in Kinsale in County Cork, far away from O'Neill's centre of power in Ulster. Mountjoy immediately laid siege to the Spaniards, preventing them from marching north. O'Neill and O'Donnell sped southwards with their army, overcoming all obstacles on their long march. On Christmas Eve, 24 December 1601, the Irish forces met Mountjoy's army in the Battle of Kinsale. The Irish, exhausted from their forced march, were overcome by the superior English forces and by the end of the battle O'Neill's dreams and ambitions for himself and Ireland lay in ruins. The Spanish surrendered and O'Neill retreated to Ulster where he held out for over a year. His power was gone however and the English forces were steadily closing in on him. He suffered a further bitter blow in 1602 when news reached him that his friend and ally, Red Hugh O'Donnell, had been poisoned in Spain. O'Donnell had fled to Spain for help after the defeat at Kinsale. Finally, with all hope lost, O'Neill sur-

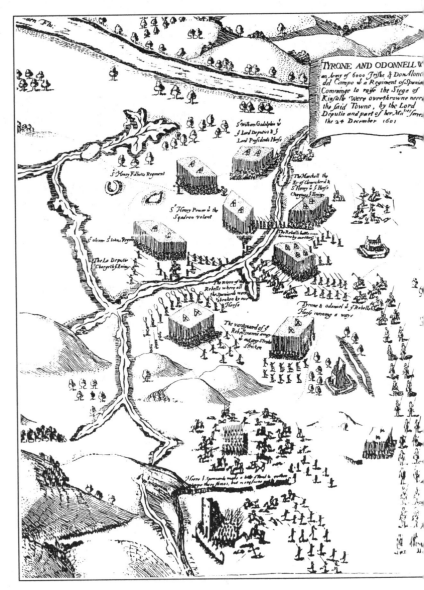

A map of the Battle of Kinsale.

rendered to Mountjoy on 30 March 1603.

Grace is thought to have died in this same year, 1603, at Rockfleet. She would probably have lived to hear of the defeat of her former friends O'Neill and O'Donnell. She would have lived therefore to witness the final extinction of the old Gaelic way of life. At the time of her birth, over 70 years before, her family and the families around her lived according to the age-old traditions of Gaelic society. Her father ruled his clan and his territory, to a large extent unaffected by the English presence in Ireland. Throughout her long life, however, Grace saw English rule spread until by the time of her death it controlled the whole country. From 1603 onwards no Irish chief ever again ruled territory and people as independently as Grace once had.

Acknowledgements

The authors and publisher thank the following for photographic material: Commissioners of Public Works pages 13, 35,48; Educational Company of Ireland 8; Bord Failte 17, 28; National Gallery of Ireland 30, 40, 51; Trinity College, Dublin 32; National Maritime Museum, Greenwich 55, 56, 57; Ulster Museum 58, 59; National Library of Ireland 65.

PLACES TO GO AND THINGS TO SEE

MAYO

The Granuaile Interpretive Centre, Louisburgh

Abbey Church, Clare Island

Kildawnet Castle

Rockfleet Castle

Burrishoole Abbey near Newport

Clare Island Castle

Westport House

DUBLIN

Howth Castle, Co. Dublin

Dublin Castle

National Museum – The De Burgo-O'Malley Chalice

National Library – papers of the period, and photographs and maps

National Gallery of Ireland

National Maritime Museum, Dun Laoghaire

Trinity College

SLIGO

Sligo Historical Society – artefacts from the Spanish Armada

CLARE

Bunratty Castle

DONEGAL

The O'Donnell Castle – Donegal town

BELFAST

Ulster Museum

Date	Granuaile	Ireland	The World
1530s	Grace O'Malley is born		Reformation continues in Europe. Emperor Charles V most powerful ruler in Europe. Spanish expeditions continue to the New World. Pizarro conquers Peru. Cortez explores California.
1531			Henry VIII forces clergy to recognise him as head of the English Church.
1534		Revolt of Silken Thomas, son of the Earl of Kildare.	Ignatius Loyola founds the Jesuit order.
1536			Michelangelo begins the 'Last Judgement' in the Sistine Chapel.
1537		Execution of Silken Thomas and his five uncles in London.	
1538		Lord Grey, Henry VIII's deputy in Ireland, the first deputy to visit the West of Ireland, receives submission from the O'Flahertys.	
1539		Dissolution of monasteries in Ireland begins.	
1540		Introduction of Surrender & Regrant policy.	
1541		Henry VIII is declared King of Ireland.	

1543		Copernicus proves the earth revolves around the sun.
1546	Grace marries Donal-an-Chogaidh.	
1549	Donal murders Walter Fada.	English *Book of Common Prayer* is ordered to be used in Ireland. Titian paints his first portraits.
1555		Philip II becomes King of Spain.
1558		Elizabeth I becomes Queen of England.
1559	Shane O'Neill becomes chieftain of the O'Neills.	
1561-7	Rebellion of Shane O'Neill	Tintoretto paints his master works.
1564	Murrough of the Battle Axes raids the Earl of Clanrickard's territory, defeats the Earl's forces. Later the Queen appoints him the O'Flaherty chieftain in place of Donal-an-Chogaidh's father.	
1565	Death of Donal-an-Chogaidh. Grace seizes Hen's Castle. Returns to Clare Island.	
1566	Grace marries Richard-an-Iarainn.	
1567	Grace's son Tibbot is born.	Shane O'Neill is murdered by the MacDonnells of Antrim. Mary Queen of Scots is forced to abdicate.
1568-73	First Desmond rebellion in Munster.	

1569		Mercator publishes a map of the world using the projection named after him.
1574	Captain Martin lays seige to Grace at Rockfleet. Grace defeats him.	
1576	First submission of an O'Malley chief to the English Lord Deputy.	Sir Edward Fitton appointed President of Connaught.
1577	Grace and Richard meet the Sidneys. Grace is captured and imprisoned by the Earl of Desmond.	Sir Nicholas Malby appointed President of Connaught. Francis Drake sets out to sail around the world.
1579	Grace is released from prison. Encouraged by the Desmond rebellion Richard-an-Iarainn, the O'Malleys and some O'Flahertys rebel.	Sir James Fitzmaurice lands with a small army at Smerwick. Earl of Desmond joins the rebellion.
1580	Grace submits to Malby. Richard-an-Iarainn becomes 'The MacWilliam', chief of the Mayo Burkes.	
1581		Galileo publishes major scientific work.
1583	Death of Richard-an-Iarainn.	Death of the Earl of Desmond. End of the Desmond rebellion.
1584	Richard Bingham appointed Governor of Connaught.	First potatoes grown in Europe.

1585		Munster Plantation.
1586	Grace arrested by Bingham. All her cattle confiscated.	
1587	Red Hugh O'Donnell captured and imprisoned.	Elizabeth executes Mary Queen of Scots.
1588		Spanish Armada.
1591	Trinity College founded in Dublin.	
1592	Red Hugh escapes from Dublin Castle.	
1593	Grace meets Queen Elizabeth.	
1594	Grace reduced to poverty from having to maintain soldiers quartered on her by Bingham.	
1595	Grace welcomes the victorious O'Donnell into Connaught.	Hugh O'Neill rebels.
1598	O'Neill and O'Donnell defeat the English at the Battle of the Yellow Ford.	
1599		Shakespeare writes *Julius Caesar*.
1601	Battle of Kinsale.	
1602	Death in Spain of Red Hugh.	
1603	Granuaile dies.	O'Neill surrenders. Elizabeth I dies.